Skein of Light

Skein of Light

poems

Karen McPherson

Airlie Press is supported by book sales and subscription orders,
by contributions to the press from its supporters,
and by the work donated by all the poet-editors of the press.

Major funding has been provided by Julia Wills.

COVER ART:
What's It Take? by Nancy Pobanz. 27″ x 55″
media: southeast Oregon raw-earth pigments
(Summer Lake Basin) and acrylic ink on watercolor paper

Cover Art Photo: Lightworks Photography

DESIGN: Cheryl McLean
AUTHOR PHOTO: Eden Parker

Airlie Press

Airlie Press
PO Box 434
Monmouth, OR 97361
editors@airliepress.org
www.airliepress.org

ISBN: 978-0-9821066-9-3
Library of Congress Control Number: 2014908818

Printed in the United States of America
Printed by Thomson-Shore on 30% postconsumer recycled paper
Processed chlorine-free

In memory of my parents
and for Elise and our children and grandchildren

CONTENTS

I

Between the real 3
Compound Fracture with Birds 4
What It Takes 5
Painstaking 6
Canning Words 7
Foregone 8
Beneath 9
Wanting 10
Joinery 11
Summer Lake Triptych 12
Walking the Beach Again 14
Art Thief 15
Biding 16
Translation in Three Movements 18
Demolition Pieces 20
Photo Shoot 22
Making the Bed 24
Disambiguation 25

II

Visiting 1978 29
Royal Quiet Deluxe 30
Wishful 31
Bantam Samplings:
Prospect Mountain Road 32
For Christopher 35
A Map of Maps 36
Ether 37
Bell, Book, and Candle 38
Middle C 40
You Change Your Name to Tom 41
My Grandmother's Collection 42

Abacus 44
Anticipating Paris 45
Lunar Eclipse 46
Precious Little Left 48
Lorca Moon 49
Kind of Blue 50
Both of Us 51

III

Timepiece III 55
Focus 56
Fugue 58
Suicide 60
Home Hospice 62
Lavender Farm 63
[aphasia] 65
As long as I have a pronoun for you 66
Veillée 68
The Day You Died 69
Crying in Public 70
Visitor 71
Some Days Are Lake 72
Openwork 74
Memento mori 76
Connecting Rooms 77
What we all long for: 78
Ballast 79
Petroglyph 80

Notes 83
Acknowledgments 85

I hear it in the deep heart's core.
—W. B. Yeats

I

Between the real

and the abstract, skirting
description (risky as landscapes
for the painter), drawn
to shadow, line, leaving
names behind, wanting
the luminous particular.

But still a language that steps out of its own way.

What will she do with the liquid warbling
of the unseen bird, the moth two days now
flat as a birthmark on the bathroom wall?

Compound Fracture with Birds

The landscape broke first
into two independent clauses.
One told of grasses sloping
under a purple martin's arabesque
to an indeterminate line of shore;
the other of the lake's shallow
burnishing interrupted by
rails wading in their own
reflections. Then the scorched mountain spoke
of red birch, wild plum, aspen
where the charcoal totems now stand.
The scorched mountain kept fracturing.

Harriers stitch the field;
cottontails lie still.
This world's sharp bones
pierce the skin of seeing.

What It Takes

Is what it gives. Stones
pried from dirt's grasp
pounded to pigment,
funneled into vials of glass—
a spectrum. Weeds
boiled, cabernet
distilled, for inks to map
the distance from this home.

There's an underbrush
of something else, a track
where insects rise
in clouds
from the wheat-
grass tide.

Just looking long
and hard enough. In balance
with the sure and measured stroke,
I find, beneath, not visible, a single
thin dark line.

Painstaking

Waking's leftover keeps me
from the landscape where I am.

Unbearably vivid,
father, mother, brother
together on the dock
—no one missing
me—no one noticing I
am missing. There's a woman
crying in a foreign tongue.
My lover says:
I don't understand what you are saying.

There's a woman I don't know
in the middle of the road,
legs splayed. She's wondering
who will help her up. All I know is
two are gone for good and one has gone
away. I've been here before,
in this foreign country without
my bag, the one with the map
and your letter.

As always, I still have my key
but can't remember what it is for.

Canning Words

She's in her studio canning
words. Calligraphed then scissored slips
drift and settle in their pectin baths. Purple
ink marbles into cat's-eye. Cool-sweated
into vacuum-sealed suspension, lining
the larder shelves, these jars whisper
reliquary. Not glassed-in coffins
for a splinter of the cross or a saint's wrinkled
fingertip, but prisms to hold
refracted, embryonic and unthreaded
in their cooling precipitate of sugar, a still
breathing piece of language.

Foregone

Can this be anything but a conclusion? Over
before it even hits the sweeping plains
of thought? Tidily wrapped in the air-
tight geometry of endpapers? Bellowing
certainty, forestalling debate, not even bothering
to wait around to exchange the usual
pleasantries? Aren't we improper even to assail it
with questions? Shouldn't we admit we
are already outstripped? Isn't it
impudent even to be thinking:

What if? What if it were instead
some hesitant scout of an idea
nosing into a thicket of possibilities?
Or else the too enthusiastic tripper of
the starting gate, hopper of mental fences
—not gone, just gone ahead?
What if it were that sparrow
on the slightest of forsythia twigs, ghosting
her own presence, her flight already imagined?

Beneath

Beneath the morning's silent listening
an evening's bells are wringing hands.
Under this ancient lakebed marshes sing

sad arpeggios. The mountains ring,
unseen, forgotten, vast expanse of sand.
Small creatures in the grass are listening

to how the harrier's thrust of wing
propels her gliding on an ample
wind just inches overhead. Blackbird sings,

watches the harrier land. In everything
there is an underside, an other hand,
something to which we are not listening.

In every turn of phrase there is a ping
of something tarnished, something contraband
we do not hear. But as I watch the willet sing

in flight and catch the pattern on her wings,
seen only from below, two vivid bands
of black and white, the morning is silent. Listening,
I hear the ancient lakebed marshes sing.

Wanting

There's a circle around what these words
cannot. The river at flood and swept with birds.
Women crossing and recrossing bridges.
In the trees, tangled nests of hair and ribbons.

That night in Dublin your hair was a dark bird,
tangled nest loosely gathered in its black ribbon.
We crossed, recrossed each bridge in widening
circles over the Liffey's flood till dawn. And now

in this other country, the trees are tangled
with birds. Women line dark nests with song.
Under the city's bridges, the river's inky ribbon
draws a tightening circle where my poem wants.

Joinery

Distracted from mitered corners
spun onto the dance floor,
my trance mimes timpani
and cymbal,
marks the time before thought
coheres. I'm loose and rich
in the house of language.

Each group of letters
is a new word, each word its own
perpetual translation.
Nothing's set yet.
Measure
by measure – dowel
matched to socket,
dadoes aligned. Fitting, splicing,
rhythms of the plane,
the endlessly circular devotions
of sand and polish.
Dovetail's
stiff fingers interlace.
Thinking comes
slowly –

like flesh,
like wood, this material moves,
ages, breathes, grows,
replicates itself.

Summer Lake Triptych

Lake

Mere sheen today across the shallow
basin, fluent stroke of light
blurred at the edges, this
April playa in late August
will become

not lake, all lakeness sucked
into its vast summer mosaic,
mud-baked hard
and raising dust
and flies.

Fire

Bare ridge recalls a single lightning
strike igniting pyroclastic air, incinerating
forests dense with ponderosa, juniper,
one hundred thousand acres scorched
in a two-week rampage.

Lakebed sucked those flames
from 7,000 feet on the valley's
downslope winds. *Not the kind of fire*
you can backburn. A pissing match
between the state and feds while
neighbors moved deliberately,
homestead to homestead,
wetting down roofs.

Wind

A wind hammering at the doors.
Its simple name will not suffice.

More than a squall, more than
a blow. Whirlwind, cyclone,
hurricane, tempest.
Such hyperbole!

It drums in time with my thudding
heart, chisels its thrill into
my shoulders. Drags me from
my bed at midnight

to press my face against
the shaking windowpane,
thinking I might see God.

Walking the Beach Again

I'm walking in the prints
I left along this moving
        edge this shimmering ragged hem
        where all sad thoughts (and glad)
        dissolve behind.

The stone I stooped to pick is smooth flat cold, my fingers
trace its curves. I'm humming at the tail of harmonies.

        A frothy surge
        wipes out the tracks ahead.

                My hand has warmed the stone;
                the stone now warms my hand.

Art Thief

for Nancy

I stole away from the studio
with that painting of yours
in my pocket. You thought
it was hanging on your wall,
but I'd already carried it off
with me in my little glasses
case. I wanted it—
so my eyes took it
and now it's
mine.

Whatever wall I turn to,
there it is.
Scribbled copper fieldscape,
thumbprint sunburned marigold,
magnified whorls and ridges
rubbed out flat.
Your *terra umbra* ground
to powder for the wind's
bold strokes. Tumbleweeds
tangled in a barbed-wire fence.

This world writes over
and over along the same horizon.
Calligraphy forest,
India paper sky.
Fluttering pages of an open book, the miracle
that reading was before you could.

Biding

This needs
a studied diffidence not to fall
defeated by the ink bottle's
gravid curve, the chattering
thesaurus, muster of pencils,
panopticon of cheering banners
push-pinned into wallboard—Miłosz
"On Prayer"; Spaar's "Widow" whose *memory*
may be an argument against this world bled nearly white
with reading; and the "Kindness" we were left with:
to learn the tender gravity of, another argument
against this world, oh, dear lost friend
and the poems with you!

Needs, too, a heart kept
open to the favored
latecomer tacked askew, hard-
chosen from those proffering
themselves: "Possibility:
An Assay"—her gift to poets,
as is possibility, I suppose,
here in a room suddenly stifling
with pause—

how else resist the usual
pileups and pentup days abstracted
from dailiness?

And needs unhurried
quiet, trust in the unobtrusive
curled in a chair,
no distinctions made
between fly and shard

as light glancing off pen catches
by a corner
waterglass and an eye—

Translation in Three Movements

Exchange

My pocket's full of change—loonies,
euros, pesos, shillings
& pence, the clink of passing
customs, crossing borders. In a row
of candy tins at home, coated in pastille
dust—guilders, pesetas, centimes,
francs. I keep old maps.

Conversion

Eureka! An unexpected vein
of hard noun nuggets and I'm that child
again who gathered words
that later became talk, and then
the world. So I become
Catholic. My Protestant
upbringing ill prepared me for
missals and lampions . . . but I'm ready
now to button myself into
this lacy Communion dress and
make my confession.

Dead Nature

Not just still but dead. A slow
death? Faded bouquets drying
in a vase, melon rotting from the inside
out? Or quick—the pheasant
already stiffening in the mastiff's jaws?
Maybe it comes when the painter pins it flat
on her gessoed board? If so, I prefer
still. A silencing, inheld breath.
But still *life*.

Demolition Pieces

Decades older than I, this pitted, crumbling bridge
and this handsome upright both can make a life-
span matter: stone and wood, iron, ivory,

and wire. The sculptor's tools are splayed
across his bench, oiled, ready for the show.

Crowds crane and gape. The showman calls: *Step*
right up! She's singing her last song. So someone

plunks a bit of "Clair de lune." And someone
else picks out a bar of "Danny Boy." We know
it's just a momentary stay. They're taking down

the old stone bridge *and none too soon*. Just yesterday,
I stood there gazing down on water muddy swift

across the rocks. Earthmovers shifting earth
and gears. Today uneasy how I, knowing, did not

know this back & forth again would be
my final in a soon-
to-be jagged gaping in the river's heart.

It's in the blueprints:
hammer to hammer, pliers

to string, mallet to wood; his tales will ease us
into the unthinkable, the jagged gaping

in the music's heart.
Struck there, we'll hang on every note,
deathwatch to wake:

music *negative* *shadow* *bridge*

Pearl Street Bridge
(1928–2009)

Milton piano
(1907–2009)

Photo Shoot

Striking
a pose I am my mother's
crooked worried smile my father
my aunt all teeth & gums unguarded
and ever conscious
of the self captured in its hairless
pink naked nervous
blink. *Look natural* – ha. Then at least try to look
out, not in.
Look out.

You could think about something
else: you're sixteen draped in sunlight
at the end of a pier you're a lone dramatic silhouette
against gray-green hills you're twirling in a field of lupine
in your favorite blue dress you are beautiful smiling
at your granddaughter a lover an appreciative
audience. The photographer is a tree, a bench
by the ocean, a kitten, a painting by Cézanne.
You are striking

from your vocabulary *leer glare*
grimace stone-faced wooden stiff
unease. Find another
language in which to be other –

though not French with its hungry
shutters and glossy spreads, its *défilés*
its *mannequins*. OK, don't think
out loud. Think lower case:
you don't really see me, *this* you don't see *this*
is who i really am
what i really look like
quickly, caught in the mirror:

oh no, it's *you*.

Making the Bed

No point, she says, we'll just
crawl in again tonight. This suit is
custom-made
for sleeping, holding our spots (you left,
me right), our human
trace, faintly flowered hint of heat
and dreams we can't remember
in the morning.
Besides, nobody comes here.

No one will see this tangled nest
woven in the sheets, so let it be
an interlude in our unbroken
hibernation, memory of the journey
shared each night in intimate
oblivion, let it wait patiently
agape until we slide back in
where we belong. I sneak back up
and make the bed.

Disambiguation

Nuance begone. Draw the line
on shades of gray. The hour
of hesitations is long
past. Decisiveness
holds sway. Though holding
sway's a danger zone as well.
Dammit to hell!

That *still* that won't hold still
and still persists in saying more
is saying more
than enough. That
that that plays with grammar
like a Tinkertoy should settle once
and for all.

For all said and done, it is.

That *like* and *as* that go around
comparing this to that in needless
complication could be struck
and nothing would be lost.

Then I could diagram this life
along a straightedge, straight and narrow
without a second thought.

II

Visiting 1978

Paid myself a visit in the old apartment on Thirteenth.
Climbed the stairs and walked right in and there I was

lying on the couch, head propped on the arm, reading
The Golden Notebook. Two flies were buzzing hard

against the screen, but I didn't seem to notice. I
kept jiggling the ice in my coffee, fiddling my braid.

When I pulled up the closest chair and leaned
across the light only then did I look up and ask me

what I was doing there. I said you have no idea
what's coming next... and I swear I did look for a minute

as if maybe I was listening, maybe even a little
curious. But my finger was keeping my place

and I'm sure I was distracted by the voices of the kids
in the parking lot and the downstairs neighbors'

stereo playing *Earth, Wind & Fire* because already I was
reading again, as if I wasn't even there. It was clear

I couldn't begin trying to imagine what I'd been
through. Become. Clear I didn't know what to do

with everything familiar I refused to see
in my own eyes. Hadn't yet anticipated

longing like this.

Royal Quiet Deluxe

With each smack and thwip I'm back with the noisy cousins
in the blueberry field's hot heavy sun next to the two
small shacks where writing's going on.

Fathers at work. Flies buzzing torn screens, clacking industry,
punctuated silences. Papers strewn, blotters
blotted, scrunched-up brows.

In the cabin kitchen blousy-aproned women fuss
at the pump. Kerosene stove. Citronella and seaweed
on a naptime wind, shhhh . . .

Matching finger's print to cold metal, then sweep
across, conducting timpani then triangle. Each carriage
returns me to the unfinished story.

Wishful

That sagging, shingled roof and dented bucket
on its rusty chain
out by the swingset at the Tipiti Motel. Tacked-up

sign: *Parents: Don't let your children lean too
far!* Even on tippy toes nothing
there to see

deep in the webby dark. Dropped our pennies in,
listened for the muffled plop,
whispered *I wish.* Just wishing

was enough. So many things to wish upon
—eyelashes, dandelion feathers, the evening
star. Successful wishes blew

away somewhere. *I wish.* No need
to specify. Even that bone, dangling
on its dish-towel hook. Clavicle, talisman,

little fork. Three weeks at least until with
pinkies crooked—the pull, bend, snap! Simple
as that. The long end got her wish,

though under the brittleness of bones
unfleshed we might have sensed promises
too fragile to be kept.

Bantam Samplings: Prospect Mountain Road

[schooling]

Ten-gallon milk cans lined up steaming
in the wooden shelter by the road for pickup,
two big neighbor boys horsing around,
one small girl, red lunchbox clutched,
buttoned-up sweater, straight-still
and watchful

after supper at the kitchen table a whole new
world of nouns
and verbs   a father's deep voice
thrilling: *puella pulchra est*
Saturday morning mother
explains the white keys and
the black, wishes we had the money
to get it tuned

[domesticating]

academia's husk cast off they burned
their lecture notes moved to the country
to raise two kids make jam read Plato trudge
to the neighbors' farm for milk, they'd practice
the domestic arts: pears wrapped in newspaper,
cucumbers fresh-dilled, grape & currant run
through cheesecloth, cowpie broth for the lettuces
and chard . . .   though later that first fall

mother at Teacher's College, daughter off to first grade,
father absorbed in his novel,
the little boy ranged his wild
kingdom undisturbed following stone walls
to where among the grazing cows
sloughed-off snakeskins crisped in the sun

[swamping]

in '55 the river rose   the basement filled
whole shelves of soggy bank slid
into the wash and all that had been clear
was loambrown frothy lapping at the skirts
of the house, furry creatures caught

the current wet backs glistened feet

made for scratching now paddled madly
turtles were swept spinning into the runoff
rivulets down steamy panes
seeped into cracks pearled up on the sills

the furnace went out—not that it mattered
all that much   the roof didn't leak
and for a joke the parents stuck a sign out
by the driveway: *Swampside*

[glistening]

what parsimonious geologist stockpiled this
shedful? what's the story behind these dense
slabs of mica piled to the roof?   Mother,
you wet your lips with a nervous tongue,
there's a patent-leather shine
on your forehead and a too bright
smile perhaps
swamping sorrow, but your children

are otherwise engaged: we pry and peel
the sheets apart with thumbs and a six-
penny nail till there are sequins
                    on our clothes and in our laps
                    windowpanes
                    of rock

For Christopher

You were wild
a tiny boy intrepid
snakecatcher
solemn explorer of stone walls
poker of cowpies.

Then you went tunnelling
into your tangled acres—we
lost it all: the bush, the berryvine,
the silver garden.

I have spent my years lavishly
unrepentant.
Now here you are.

Brother.
Some kid I knew in the old
neighborhood.

Cracked and mended.
There's always a seam.
We can feel it.

A Map of Maps

for my grandfather, the geographer

Childhood was a mischief of maps,
coded imaginings on every wall—
quilts of the prairie states, Wabash
calabash, scrawl of river lace
Sault Ste. Marie to the Missouri
confluence, periscopic contourings
of range and ridge and rim,
graded blues to the oceans'
deepest troughs, crosshatched
elevations of tectonic plates and slides.

The Mississippi Delta spilled
into my bathtub. Climbing
the stairs a History of the West
1830 to 1910. Above the guestroom
dresser, Antarctica—misshapen
dinner plate in alabaster,
tiny black names etched
around its chipped and fluted edge.

Being anywhere meant standing
on a map. Eyes were compasses,
arms protractor, spine and shoulders
straightedge, theodolite,
in a back pocket always a notebook
for the legends and the scale.

A child could get lost as long as she
had a map to draw the tracings
of that errancy. Men made them.
But a girl could set out:
Deep South, Far East, True North.

Ether

They're feeding me
the liquid air of flowers
through a thin straw of glass.

I'm a hard drop of light
drawn into the tunnel:
poison flowers.

They're spinning me
the flowers' sweet-smelling
light deep into glass-blown chambers.

On paper trays, sharp glass. I'm still
in the body. Under flowers. Heavy light.
I'm only five and there's a glass

and there's a light.

Bell, Book, and Candle

In the 9th century those who committed
particularly grievous sins were
excommunicated, bell, book, and candle.

Nothing so dire.
A nursery rhyme: *Ding dong bell . . .*

The one my mother had was
small and brass, shaped like a woman
in a long, full skirt. You
could pick her up by the head
and shoulders, jiggle her
a little, and that skirt
would ring.

It's mine now, the bell,
and so's the candle-
stick, brass as well with a small,
curved handle for your finger
and a clever snuffer
fitted in the stem. The kind
of candlestick you'd carry up the stairs
to light you to bed . . .

In the village near the village
where I grew up, the bookshop
was called *The Hickory Stick*. I got my
Puffin books there, rousing stories of
intrepid English boys and girls, their
cheeky humour with a *u*,
their boarding schools and
bachelor uncles.

The French have a lovely
word for it: *chevet*. On my
nightstand now there's a grown-up
book I'm reading at a glacial
pace, my mother's little
bell, and in the brass candlestick
a candle I never light,
afraid of dying
in my bed.

Middle C

She's been holding the center since I
was five, the year my mother tried to teach me.
Anchoring my attention then—and my right
index finger—like Home

in a game of Tag. She made particular sense
to me, not like the inscrutable others,
foreign, narrow-shouldered crowd
in their identical black&white jackets
mumbling up and down the alphabet.

Propped in front of me
that tadpole map—
this wasn't like books where eyes
could race ahead at the tail of some marvelous
adventure. These letters didn't spell
anything. There was a secret
code, but it was something fingers
had to learn. I wasn't good at

not being good at things.
I grew anxious, my teacher lost patience.
The starting point became the coda.

Though there she is still in the pitch
perfect center, vibrant to my glance.

You Change Your Name to Tom

At fifty-six you've stepped at last out of your
latest novel and into your own life, all the family
fictions in your wake.

Tell me, was everything before a travesty
since now you're dressed in your own
authentic skin?

To me you were always that boy without
a face, the one imagining himself:
The Man in the Iron Mask.

Always in your world I sensed myself other
than my given name. The two
who named us are no longer here.

So tell me, who are we now?

My Grandmother's Collection

Tiger Cowry, Lettered Olive, Pacific Conch—storybook
names penned lovingly in an inked cerulean
script now faded pink.

Her brother, childless man, with means and more
to hire the native diver—Bora Bora, Vanuatu—finance
marine plunder for his Cincinnati museum,

brought her back treasures
with Latin names. The Chambered Nautilus was,
she said, most rare. I knelt beside her

at the altar where that light-filled
chalice lay curved
around its hidden spaces.

Yet more, I think, she prized the ones she lifted
from the sand herself on Sanibel
or Myrtle Beach, days when the wind

was down, *tic douloureux* not keeping her
confined to shaded rooms. Those subtle winks
and dabs of color spied on a canvas

of sand. She'd stiffly squat
to ease them free; each tiny shell admired
on open hand then pocketed.

When I was snorkeling off Ambergris,
dazzled by exotic beauties far beyond my reach,
I thought of him. But kneeling now

to pick a perfect cockle from
the shell hash near Ocracoke,
I think of her.

Abacus

Spell it out. All understanding
is phonetic. Our first texts—Braille and light—
were listing towers.

Everything fit. From A to B
to sing along with me. In grammar school,
even the exceptions were ruled
by rules.

We lay straight as pins between the dotted lines,
casting our spells with abracadabras.

Sound it out. A single letter
can be a person. Two
for making sense. Three for
sentences. Four for lies.

We had it figured out
along a wire and frame. One equals
one. Each satisfying click of
black and white, a calculus.

Now every handmade shift in my color-coded closet
is trying to dress up what you mean to say.

Anticipating Paris

At a distance the city becomes cliché:
avenues lined with broad-leafed chestnuts,
stiletto staccatos on the metro stairs,
toy sailboats foundering in the Luxembourg
fountain. A boulangerie on every corner,
a pack of Gauloises in every pocket,
a ten-dollar café crème at every tourist-
trap terrasse along the Champs-Élysées.

Up close I found the city was still
cliché: metropolis built on bones. Its roots
in the catacombs and sewers. Barely twenty, I
threaded my way across a dozen picturesque
bridges clogged with backpackers
and buskers. Crossed the map to climb and catch
a breather among the dead and the hungry
feral cats at Père-Lachaise.
Barely thirty, I penned a bad poem in equally
bad French at a corner table at the Café de Flore,
paused reverently in the street outside 27
rue de Fleurus. Paris in the eighties was still Paris
in the thirties.

And now, a woman in her sixties, I cannot stop
anticipating Paris. Thin penciled eyebrows
raised in disdain, rows of candles guttering
in cathedral dark, poets in cramped garret rooms,
even the daemon lover in her galleries of glass.

Lunar Eclipse

April 1996 for H

There's no way to know
where it is not, or scan
the vast expanse of sky

to find its absence.

Each of us in this crowd
by the playing fields
has come to contemplate
this disappearance
to penetrate
what is not there
until at last

it is: in imagination first
memory of moons
idea of a globe
then slow red developing

a negative moon rises
from its nightblue bath.

Thirty minutes more
before scalpel
of light
cuts through.

Watching the thin sharp
crescent quiver, I am
remembering the moon
that earlier in that place
was not there

and the friend in Cape Town
who yesterday
had not yet died.

Precious Little Left

A smudge across the tattered
corner of a photograph, a few
addresses scribbled
on an ink-stained blotter, some
doors ajar, half-open
cupboards

  disquieting murmurs

    everything but the chalk outline . . .

I'm collecting
flakes of skin
alibis strung together
worry beads
ugly rumors
whatever's necessary
for the final accounting.

I'm tucking reminders
theories, syntax
into tiny hinged boxes

  making sentences.

Lorca Moon

for G

Firestorm of stars, we two girls
seventeen on the pond's grassy bank
whispering suicide and melon
moons, passions
neither of us had known—but for you
the lust of razor blades was real,
padlocked cabinets, patient father
walking the halls
outside your mother's room.

I was so normal, my uncomplicated family, all that
good New England forthrightness. I wanted
your exotic anguish. We tortured every word,
bled into each other's mouths and ears and one night
you said you would carve & drown and another
night you did & nearly did and left your calling card
for me.

Late summer when I left
that pond behind, you still in the shallows,
you were older than I
would ever be.

Kind of Blue

after Miles Davis

Slow bass thrumming to a hardtack
shoreline where burnt-sugar grasses riff
the kettle hills. Look up! A high manuscript
is signing as inkspots gather, pull as one
over the southern horizon.

Improv. Spectrum plays chromatic
scales. Umber and cadmium nudge
the borders. A rock is a bird is a rock.
In the Andes a weaver names the constellations:
llama and *cria*, fox and condor.

That sharp white line cuts this world
in two. Last evening one thick blue stroke
made us see the ocean. Now rock
striations, penciled grasses impose the weft
and warp, and I wait at the loom.

Something comes into our sleep.
There is an ocean underneath
this desert. And a desert underneath
that ocean. *Unutterably sad,* she said, where she lay
in the cradle of a fallen, burned-out juniper.

When you close your eyes, the land will hold you.

Both of Us

I wasn't there. You were. And maybe that's
the why of it, what I *was not holding,*
what was slipping—in that quiet inheld moment—away,
from both of us. I'm needing the world to be still

suppertimes and slippers. Your chewed-up
nails, your penmanship the teacher called
appalling, those ever-reassuring rituals of
our quarreling. I want that time before, again,

the day you let me come along behind you single
file on that slick log across the Aspetuck.
Brooks running snowmelt. I loved you, in your kingdom,
like someone's darling. Tiny waterfalls,

pastel lichen shelves, rainbow mist of dragonflies,
and coral bells. You promised and we shared that secret
place like a handshake. Now I've been looking west
for years whenever you look east.

Our children now have children our mother
never knew. I don't want to feel what I've been
feeling, want to find you in this shimmering we've
forgotten, the question I've been afraid to ask. *Was I there?*

Tell me I was there.

III

Timepiece III

mixed media in black, silver, & white
by M. Reynolds

Grief-bowed mother, mantel clock's
round face. Casement framing hieroglyphs
of worry, scribbled

heartbeat, a night in silver
wash. To trace the twinning scratches
of another indecipherable

story, my eyes are fingertips.
Shiny metal backdrop might be
raining   prayerfulness

or merely eyes veiled in the unfocused
half-light, a flaw on the surface
of the glass.

In this mirror my hair is white,
my mother is dead,
the lines go nowhere.

Focus

Field glasses trained
first pin that blur
to wagging branch.

Minute adjustments guide
image to one silhouette.
Mind

zeroes in: *redwing blackbird*. Fine-
tuning after years. Time was,
these two

wanted each to go its way,
tempted by some flashing
at the hem of sight.

Doctors clipped their wings,
determined they should work
and play together.

Exercises in the stereoscope: one bird,
one blue balloon, one boy,
one girl. Inevitably

the left one tired and drooped when
looking got too hard, the other
always lazy.

Came a time a letter *would*
stand upright on the page,
stylus-sharp,

and shifting worlds settled
into singular depths.
And yes, a point

when thinking did the same,
even in private, behind
shuttered doors.

Trying to unfocus now, forget
the name. See it all
at once, unframed.

Fugue

Attending.

Reckoning how long.
Murmurings and silence
crowding the hallways.
Fingers caught in hair
longing and lengthening—
pin drop.

The Bleed.

Madras flows in violet
chemical wash
one instant
fixed in silver
phantom images
when you spike a vein.

Sustaining.

Resonant bass. Calamity
at bay. Growing this inkling
star holding whole villages
in a lungful of air
under the gentle, under the steady
pressure of a pedal.

The Wake.

As if
in a single morning
grape hyacinth narcissus
flowering quince
in a single night—snow
like ash
across a buried city.

Will you?

Diminishing.

My own (distancing)
outgrown yet through
upended glass all is still
crystal
a detail
of a detail chiseled
perfect.

Punctum.

What is, is not.
Your mischief on glossy paper
fools me out of time. Heat
ricochets around an empty room. We miss
the cooling. The departure. The sudden
vacancy. A textured thumbprint. A pulse
no longer ticking. You are retinal.

Suicide

acrylics on canvas by M. Reynolds

This must be where Icarus fell. Shadows
trim the owl's kite-wings. No breath
in this unforgiving spot.

That bird hovered over my mother's chair
while she sank into stone. Was she less
alone under those outspread wings? I can only guess

what story she saw waiting for her there,
but didn't see, the scene forever
at her back, drawing her in to what she was not facing.

Two wide-eyed windows carved
in the palisade, plummeting
off the canvas edge while

in the lamprey jungle down below, in
weedy shadows on the valley floor,
is that a spot of blood?

Or someone's cigarette? A signal lit, perhaps,
before the light gave out, made him forget?
Whose suicide is this? The painter is

inscrutable. But *someone* had to build
that long stone flight climbing
the headlands to the sun each afternoon.

Granite heavy on his shoulders, was he
trudging, humming, breaking for a smoke
halfway up? Pleasures for the taking.

She curled into her armchair as language went away.
The sleep of children, mouth agape. Later
we hired a man to build a crate, cart off

this memory of her traipsing up that long stone
stair to where I now can see the missing beach,
her final walk into the sea.

Home Hospice

We mill about and hover,
pick up dishes, answer phones,
a crowd of extras, supporting cast, blocking scenes,
memorizing lines
ever the same ever different as if different
intonations might make better
sense, better use of little time, clutching
stained and dog-eared
scripts so nearly unreadable
we think they must be
familiar but not

what to say:
Hold my hand. Count with me. Measuring pain
and breaths, pain and breaths as the dailiness
of dying curiously resembles
the dailiness of living

then unaccustomed mirth as someone
opens a window and napkins fly off the table
like pigeon ghosts alighting on the rug in papery ballet
fallen wings one gathers gently up and smooths back
into neatly folded squares

Lavender Farm

for Melva

She spends her days mostly
on the hillside.

There are no doors on the hillside
no empty beds no clatter of dishes
no coats let drop in the hallway no
shouts down the stairs. Only Hidcote,
Royal Velvet, Munstead, Dark Eyes.

The younger boy, the one
who didn't die, headed out east in early spring.
He's living reckless there,
she's sure—he doesn't call,
maybe once a month. Too sad her all alone
after the marriage's unuttered conversation
deepened grief, could not withstand
their need for not
keeping company.

Daily now
she solves the puzzle
of irrigation & drainage, maps the pattern
of path & gate, kneels so the sun can
soften her shoulders.

By the sundial, in the busyness of bees,
she crushes a sprig of Provence
between finger and thumb, inhales
as though she might breathe in whole

the golden heat, the whorl of butterflies, as if
in that pause
she might hold his breath
as they stand atop the rock, joyously eighteen,
arms spread and grinning
in that triumphant moment before the dive.

[aphasia]

First names drop out, their gleaming capitals afire,
a nimbus alphabet of hints and dread, of ends quickly
scrawled onto scraps, a bold tattoo, mocking singsong
marshaling the search, a calling out of letters that do
yet do not correspond to any place I've known.

Again, again that flashing neon cross-
town on a rooftop, my GPS, my angel guide. Again,
again bend down to jam the three prongs in. They
spark and make the hairs stand up and lo,
at first the shape of something flares.

But roaring soon subsides into a sniff.
Jellies and schist. No ticking pulse, the still form
must be shocked again.

While in another room it tucks my bed with promises
to settle at last into its rightful whole. Always another
room, more promises, and try too many times, even
the capitals are gone. *Jellies and schist?* I catch
a glance of heat and light, the hole they leave in space,
but no letter there where saying was. No letter.
Only a face—always a face—

As long as I have a pronoun for you

returning happens
until only the new

tight green lilac
bud in its perfect bead
of ice

tells of any change
in pattern or step
from year

one standing still
in shock before
the ironed altarcloth

to year and though I've turned
all the calendars
to the wall

two and three times
the alternating freeze
and thaw

you're always leaving, left
behind as memory
stretches her unbreakable wire

bound up in first remembering
then forgetting this, exquisite
tightrope act, needle

piercing to gather days
months years until—stitched through
the seasons' repetitions—it's

winter again on your Chinese plate
above my mantel
and on all the other graftings

a precious weight always, yet ever
too little in harvests

and unexpected springs.

Veillée

the light comes from the dark inside
the light comes
from the heavy
dark stone in my lap
as I sing
lullabies
I thought forgotten every
breath a stitching
folded in a jacket we thought forgotten
every breath measured waves
lapping our lungs
walls and flesh translucent

the cyclone
that fades from your eyes into mine
and the weight that shines
from inside the dark

The Day You Died

for my father

I stepped aside discreetly for a moment's
visit to my life and in that moment quietly
you took leave of yours

as if to give a blessing to that turn from
loss, as if to say there's room for both
the living and the dying and each

shall go her way or his as natural and
as planned. I took your hand, you let me
go, you let me stay.

Crying in Public

Once running through the walking streets,
jostling Parisian crowds across the Pont
des Arts—after he'd gone
off with a cheerful girl
from Delaware.

Once in the Japanese Garden,
leaning over looking into
the face below the bridge, my own
nineteen-year-old
misery.

Once on an eastbound bus near Winnipeg,
forehead pressed to cold glass
measuring thousands of snowy miles
behind, between me
and before.

Once at the Canadian border,
serious young woman in uniform
asking *business or pleasure?*
In my suitcase
a small cardboard box of ashes.

Visitor

Silently from every side
they step into the clearing to feed.
I imagine this is how angels would come.

The one closest to the window knows
I'm here. Her still gaze meets mine
and holds. She's looking
into my look, to the wild
quiet somewhere deeper.

Sun slants across snowdrifts.
Frozen landscape flits with chickadees
nuthatches a splash of cardinal.

Last evening we two old friends stretched
into the woodfire comfort
of talk or silence
until a second vodka brought everything
burning back.

Letting ourselves remember, we sensed us each
at the clearing's edge, knew us each intently
focused on the place of missing
between us, the pinpoint spot of longing,

until in that holographic intersection
—like sun magnified to pierce
a leaf with its needle of fire—
we invited her in   and suddenly
she was there.

Some Days Are Lake

Some days are lake, some light
across a shattered mud-
caked flat. One minute I'm on land,
the next on water. No clean edge
to this striated world. Colors make
depth where light makes plane. I look again:

the cranes are back on the far hill again,
hard to discern against this skein of light.
But through field glasses I can make
them out quite well. Later I scrape the mud
I've brought up from the playa's edge
caked to my boots. The purple martins land

and lift, and lift and land,
the redwing blackbird calls again
from somewhere near the meadow's edge.
The painters catch this light
in little jars, gather up dust and mud,
the bones of trees, and out of these make

generous worlds, while I make
pencil-scrapings of this land
and sky, slim scansions of grass, mud
clinging to my rubber boots again.
I'm hopeful, walking down into the light
of another morning on the edge

of this, a world where painters have an edge.
Marveling how in tinctures they will make
their pigments into light
and then with brushes spread the land-
scape out across abstraction. Again
the clouds are treetops, birds are mud.

I, too, keep straining through this mud
to try to stand upon the very edge
of saying something new, again.
Might this be what it is to make
a poem? One foot on land,
one in the water, eyes closed against the light?

Is it this caking mud that makes
me, edging my way across a land-
scape, heavy with images, so light?

Openwork

Between us spreading
rivers   unfinished
sentences   disappearing
prairies   and I

work my way
deliberately   (joyfully!)
through lattices of silence
into an opening
narrow as a seam
of light . . .
            tunnel into
            where I thought
            I left you where I
            find now only

            this warm current
            of your passage.

                        There's a way
    you move your head
    to brush aside
    whatever speaking does

a way you say
don't say
and then I don't.

But days like this
I almost taste your thoughts

days like this I think
I might say
anything.

Memento mori

The Victorians took photographs
of the stillborn child.

Aligned here on the hillside's
flattened grass, burned-out plates of light contain
the shattering.

Nine salvaged windows,
blueprint for a glass
house. Cloudless mirrors ready
for the raising. Fire rose instead.

Furious wind and flame
along the ridge. When the sap
reached a boil, the trees exploded
in Catherine wheels.

Blistered frames blazed and
were consumed. Panes
shattered in place, their shards
fused into prismic shapes, hold

the idea of tender seedlings to be
watched and watered
through the long, dry summer.

Connecting Rooms

These days I don't always visit
the still and sunlit room where I am missing
you *all the time.* Days pass and days and I
pass the door knowing it would take a fingertip
to push it wide, a step to find myself
inside that place. Wind thunders brain to blood
against the chamber wall as I do not enter

this or those connecting
rooms beyond – stilled beads along a silent rosary
now confided in the folds of bright
receding spaces, voices sealed in amber
lockets I have not the heart

to open.

What we all long for:

but no list follows   as if
the world itself would
answer in its spaciousness

as if a sunbright tide or forest
perfume compensate
the commonplace of loss

unhinge the frame unfurl
the peacock curtains
cast caution and desire

to earth to seed to sow

Ballast

Loosestrife worries cast off their clouds of seed.

News from away, alarming how unprepared
I am for this disturbance
to the meadow. Losses,

heavy pennies. I gather myself in, siphon off
graywater—these scorched forests,
dwindling summers.

Out on the shallow lake, we're riding low.

Furiously, I haul in every trick of light
and birdsong I can net
                    to keep afloat.

Petroglyph

Unlabelled, crammed into cabinets,
letters from people I know as a
story
told too many times.

Have I kept them because she was
a girl I am and may still want
to love? Oh sure,

posterity makes sense
when you are young. But now
with the novel's pages few enough

to want to slow the reading down,
I can
imagine not wanting
to be where I no longer am.

This wind-stripped valley shears
all new each day. Easy to embrace
one's absence in the world.

Though off the trail, comfort
in a telegraphic human trace
scratched into a gray rock's face.

NOTES

"Between the real"

Donald Hall writes of Jane Kenyon studying "the art of the luminous particular."

"What It Takes"

After the painting *What's It Take?* by Nancy Pobanz.

"Canning Words"

After the 2009 art installation by Michelle Danforth (Mason canning jars, pectin, white wine, paper, and ink).

"Summer Lake Triptych"

In July 2002, the Winter Ridge and Toolbox fires joined forces to burn more than ninety-two thousand acres of forest along the west side of Summer Lake near Paisley, Oregon.

"Demolition Pieces"

A new Pearl Street Bridge crosses the Gihon River in Johnson, Vermont. Michael Frassinelli dismantled the Milton piano in his studio on July 5, 2009.

"Bantam Samplings: Prospect Mountain Road"

Bantam is a borough in Litchfield County in northwestern Connecticut.

"Bell, Book, and Candle"

A traditional English nursery rhyme begins: "Ding dong bell, pussy's in the well. Who put her in? Little Johnny Flynn." Another English children's game called "Oranges and Lemons" ends with the lines: "Here comes a candle to light you to bed, and here comes a chopper to chop off your head." The name of the Hickory Stick Bookshop in Washington, Connecticut, probably comes from a line in the 1907 popular American song "School Days": "Reading and 'riting and 'rithmetic, taught to the tune of a hickory stick."

"[aphasia]"

"While it is true that as we age . . . nominal aphasia (the ability to remember names and words) worsens, this does not foreshadow sinister events." —Mary Grogan, "The Secrets of Ageing Well"

Acknowledgments

Grateful acknowledgment is made to the publications in which these poems first appeared, sometimes in different form:

Umbrella: "Foregone"
Passager: "Visiting 1978"
Cider Press Review: "Joinery"
Potomac Review: "Art Thief"
Paper Nautilus: "A Map of Maps"
Beloit Poetry Journal: "What It Takes"
Sketching Elise (Finishing Line Press): "Wanting" and "Openwork"

My deepest gratitude to Liz Ahl for incisive readings and encouragement and to Nancy Pobanz for the cover image. Thank you as well to the Airlie Press editors for their generosity and editorial guidance. This book was nourished by the friendship and inspiration of the Porch Sisters (Liz Ahl, Kathy Sheeder Bonanno, Nancy Welch, and Susan Lilley) and the Playa sisters (Nancy Pobanz, Joan Stuart Ross, Rakar West, and Nina Elder). The Wicked Good Writers (who *are*) have kept me company and kept me writing. Thanks also to Vermont Studio Center and Playa for residencies that gave me the gift of time and space to complete this book.

About the Publisher

Airlie Press is run by writers. A nonprofit publishing collective, the press is dedicated to producing beautiful and compelling books of poetry. Its mission is to offer writers working in its particular habitat a local, shared-work publishing alternative. Airlie Press is supported by book sales, subscription orders, and donations. All funds return to the press for the creation of new books of poetry.

Other Titles from Airlie Press

Donna Henderson *The Eddy Fence*
Jessica Lamb *Last Apples of Late Empires*
Anita Sullivan *Garden of Beasts*
Carter McKenzie *Out of Refusal*
Cecelia Hagen *Entering*
Chris Anderson *The Next Thing Always Belongs*
Stephanie Lenox *Congress of Strange People*
Annie Lighthart *Iron String*
Dawn Diez Willis *Still Life with Judas & Lightning*
Tim Shaner *Picture X*

Colophon

Titles and text are set in Book Antiqua, a font developed by Microsoft to replicate the classic font Palatino, designed by Hermann Zapf and released in 1948 by Linotype.